**Managing Editor**
Karen J. Goldfluss, M.S. Ed.

**Editor-in-Chief**
Sharon Coan, M.S. Ed.

**Illustrators**
Howard Chaney
Bruce Hedges

**Cover Artist**
Lesley Palmer

**Art Coordinator**
Kevin Barnes

**Art Director**
CJae Froshay

**Imaging**
Temo Parra

**Product Manager**
Phil Garcia

**Publisher**
Mary D. Smith, M.S. Ed.

# Insects

## SUPER SCIENCE ACTIVITIES

*Written by Ruth M. Young, M.S. Ed.*

Teacher
Created
Resources

***Teacher Created Resources, Inc.***
6421 Industy Way
Westminster, CA 92683
wwwteachercreated.com

*©2002 Teacher Created Resources, Inc.*
Reprinted, 2005
Made in the U. S. A.
**ISBN-0-7439-3661-2**

# Table of Contents

# Introduction

Insects are found all over the world, even in Antarctica. They have been on Earth at least 400 million years and appear to be in no danger of disappearing in the future. There are more insects and more kinds of insects than all other animals on Earth which are visible to the naked eye. Insects have been called man's worst enemy, but this is not true. It is important to respect their role in the balance of nature and know that most life on Earth could not exist without them. Insects are an important food source for many animals, they are pollinators of many commercial plants, they are garbage collectors, and they are silk weavers. They are gems of natural beauty and a constant source of interest.

Insects have an outside skeleton (*exoskeleton*), six legs, and three body parts. Compare the physical features of the insect to crabs and lobsters, and you can see that they are related. Insects also may have one or two pairs of wings attached to the middle section of the body (*thorax*). They usually have two sets of jaws, two kinds of eyes (simple and compound), and one pair of antennae. There are exceptions to these physical features, however. Some insects have a thorax and abdomen which seem to run together. Immature stages (*larvae*) of many insects look like jointed worms with six real legs and perhaps some extra false ones.

Another confusion comes about due to animals which look like insects. These include spiders and scorpions, but they have too few body parts (two) and too many legs (eight). Crustaceans (e.g., crabs, lobsters, and shrimp) also look like insects but may have five pairs of legs and two pairs of antennae. Sowbugs and pillbugs are land crustaceans. Centipedes and millipedes have many segments to their bodies with one pair of legs (in the case of centipedes) or two pairs (in the case of millipedes) attached to each segment.

The study of insects begins with a hunt on the school grounds and a pretest to separate insects from noninsects. As students continue the activities in this section, they will learn about insects by raising mealworms, ants, butterflies, and silkworms in the classroom. As a culminating activity, students will create imaginary insects for their own insect zoo.

# Going on an Insect Hunt

## *Gathering Specimens*

**Overview:** *Students will gather specimens of insects and noninsects.*

## Materials

- 3" x 5" (8 cm x 13 cm) unlined file cards
- 1" (2.5 cm) cube plastic bug boxes with a magnifying lid (See Delta Education in Resources.)
- snack-sized resealable bag
- parent letter for insects (page 5)
- overhead projector with transparencies of insects and noninsects (See Closure.)

## Lesson Preparation

- Take a walk around the grounds near the school, searching for insects and noninsects. Look in hidden places such as on plants, under fallen leaves, and along tree bark.
- Map a route for the students to take as they search for specimens during this activity.

## Activity

1. Distribute a file card to each student and ask each one to draw an insect on it. Tell students to make their pictures as large as the card. Let them know that you want them to show as many details of the insect as they can, including the shapes of the body parts and legs.
2. Have the students show their drawings to others and point out the details, such as legs.
3. Tell the students that they are going on an insect hunt around the school ground. Take them to the search area and distribute a magnifying box to each student. Explain that they are to find only one insect to place in the box and then bring it to a central location you establish. You may wish to use a signal to call them back together after a set time.
4. When the students have each found an insect, gather them together and look at what they have found. Let the students exchange magnifying boxes to look closely at their insects. If any have placed noninsects in their boxes, do not correct them at this time.

## Closure

- Return to the classroom and select examples of the insects to see enlarged on the overhead projector. Place an insect in a resealable bag on the projector stage. Have students point out its physical features (e.g., number of legs, body parts, and shape). (*Note:* The heat from the projector will affect the insect, so it should not be subjected to the light for long periods.)
- Have the students draw their insects on the other side of the card they used at the beginning of the class period. Collect these cards to use as assessment at the end of this lesson series.

## Homework

Send home a copy of the parent letter with a small resealable bag stapled to it.

# Going on an Insect Hunt *(cont.)*

### *Parent Letter for Insect Hunt*

Date_____

**Dear Parents,**

We are studying insects in science. Today we began our study by having each student make a drawing of an insect. Then we all took a walk around the school grounds, with each student collecting an animal he or she thought was an insect. We looked at these with magnifying lenses and the overhead projector to make them larger and easier to see their details. The students then drew the insects they had collected.

The next step in our study is for each student to capture an insect in his or her yard and bring it to school tomorrow. After we have examined these insects, they will be released in the school yard.

You will find a small resealable bag attached to this note. Please help your child capture an insect to put inside the plastic bag and bring it back to school tomorrow for our science class. Since we are just beginning our study of insects, your child may choose an animal which looks like an insect but is not really a true insect. It is important that children discover the differences for themselves, so please do not tell them if their choice is not an insect.

Tomorrow, we will look at the specimens the children bring to class. We will also compare the specimens with the drawings children have made of the insects they found on our insect hunt today.

Be sure to ask your child about the experience today and ask him or her to draw a picture below of the insect collected today.

## Today's Insect

Thank you for helping your child find an interesting insect to bring to school.

Cordially,

_____

# Is This an Insect?

### *Insects and Noninsects*

**Overview:** *Students will learn to distinguish insects from noninsects.*

## Materials

- transparency and copies of page 7
- insects students bring from home
- 3" x 5" (8 cm x 13 cm) unlined file cards and magnifying boxes
- overhead projector with transparencies of Outside Parts of Insects and Inside Parts of Insects (pages 8 and 11)

## Lesson Preparation

- Gather examples of noninsects (e.g., spider, pill bug, millipede) to use with the students.
- Collect insect specimens students bring and place them in magnifying boxes. Put them where they can be viewed by students before beginning the class.

## Activity

1. Distribute file cards and insects in magnifying boxes. Have students draw their own specimens. Give them the pictures made yesterday to look for differences and likenesses.
2. Show students' specimens in resealable bags on the overhead projector.
3. Distribute copies of page 7 and have students circle the letters of those they think are insects. Show the transparency of page 7 and have students vote on which ones they think are insects. Circle the letters for those they choose.
4. Use the transparency of page 8 (Outside Parts of Insects) and explain. Place examples of insects in a zip-lock bag (one at a time) to show on the overhead. Let students see if they can find six legs and three body parts. Use several examples of noninsects to show differences from insects.

## Closure

- Show the transparency of page 7 again and ask students to vote once more on which are examples of insects. Ask them to point out details which help find real insects. Tell them the names of the insects and noninsects on this sheet.

| *Insects* | | *Noninsects* |
|---|---|---|
| B. silverfish | G. grasshopper | A. scorpion |
| C. ant | I. butterfly | F. tarantula (spider) |
| D. stag beetle | K. cockroach | H. centipede |
| E. earwig | L. butterfly larva | J. millipede |

- Place live examples of insects and noninsects on the overhead projector. Have students write which ones they think are insects. Collect the papers, review the specimens, and let students vote aloud. If there is disagreement, have them explain what made them decide how to vote. Tell them the correct answers.

# Is This an Insect? *(cont.)*

## *Insect Identification*

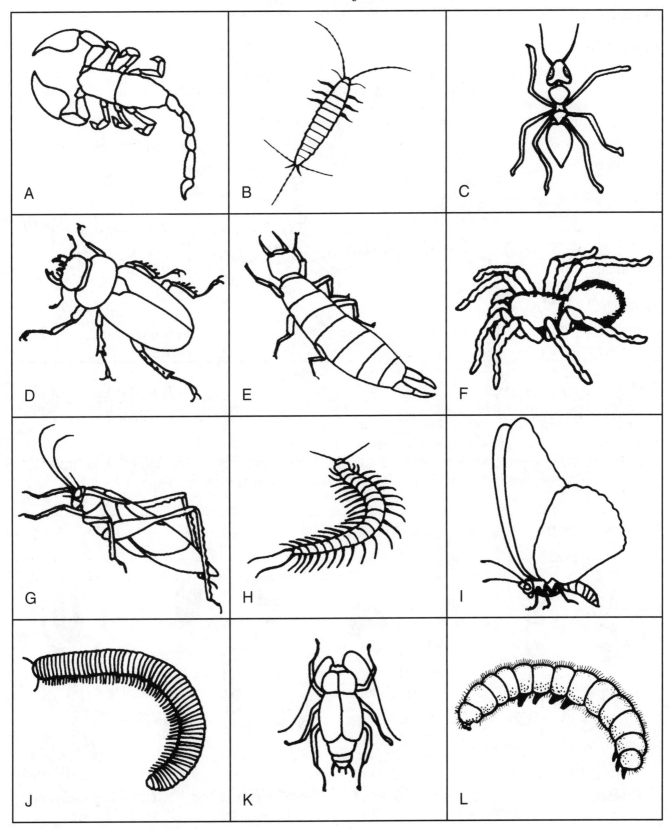

# Is This an Insect? *(cont.)*

## *Outside Parts of Insects*

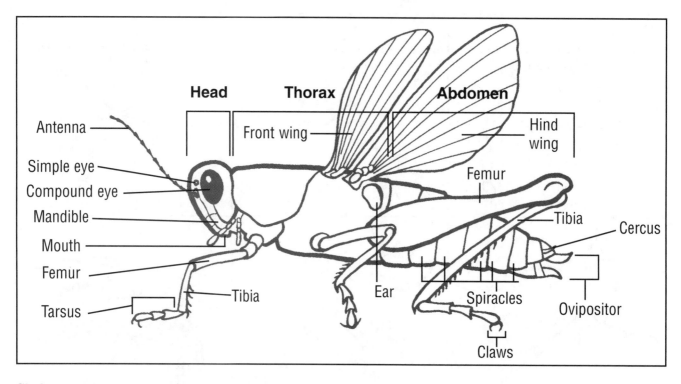

**Skeleton:** The insect's skeleton is outside of its body and is called an *exoskeleton*. It is like a suit of armor that protects the soft internal parts. It is divided into three parts—*head*, *thorax*, and *abdomen*. The muscles are attached to the inside wall of this exoskeleton.

The insect's three body parts are described below and on pages 9 and 10.

A. **Head:** There are five or six segments to an insect's head, but they are too tightly packed together to be seen separately. The head is made up of the *mouthparts*, *eyes*, and *antennae*.

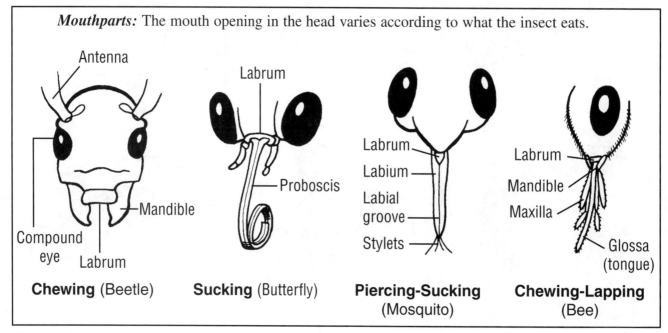

*Mouthparts:* The mouth opening in the head varies according to what the insect eats.

**Chewing** (Beetle)  **Sucking** (Butterfly)  **Piercing-Sucking** (Mosquito)  **Chewing-Lapping** (Bee)

### *Outside Parts of Insects (cont.)*

**A. Head:** *(cont.)*

*Eyes:* Most adult insects have two large bulging compound eyes on either side of their heads. These are made up of separate lenses, sometimes thousands of them. Each lens sees a piece of the image, and these pieces combine to form a mosaic. This is not a very clear image, but because of the shape of the eyes, the insect can see up, down, ahead, and back at the same time. This type of eye is especially good for seeing motion. Many insects also have smaller, single-lens eyes. These can see only light and dark, not an image. Insects have different color ranges than humans, mostly seeing only green, blue, and ultraviolet.

*Antennae:* Almost all insects have two antennae between their eyes. These are used mostly to smell and to feel. Some insects also use these to taste and to hear. The antennae are segmented and flexible, appearing in various shapes.

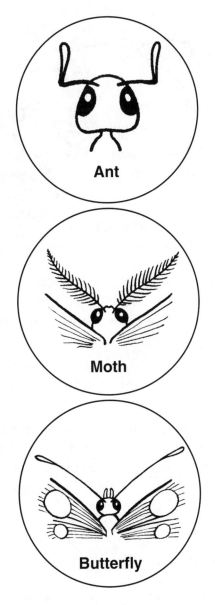

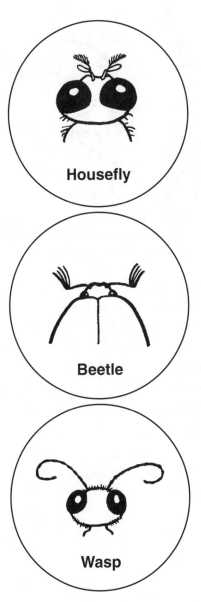

### *Outside Parts of Insects (cont.)*

**B. Thorax:** The wings and legs are attached to this middle section of the body, which consists of three tightly fused segments. Most adult insects have wings. A single pair of wings is attached to the middle segments. If there are two pairs of wings, they are attached to the middle and last segments of the thorax.

The six legs are attached in pairs to each segment of the abdomen. The legs each have five main sections with movable joints between them. Legs are often adapted for swimming, digging, or jumping. Honeybees have pollen-collecting baskets on their hind legs. The front legs of butterflies are small, hairy, and often have special organs for finding food. Feet may have hooks and sticky pads (e.g., flies and bees) to help them hold to slippery surfaces or walk upside down.

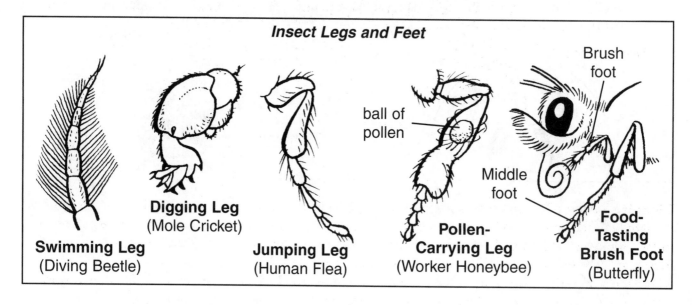

**Insect Legs and Feet**

Swimming Leg (Diving Beetle)

Digging Leg (Mole Cricket)

Jumping Leg (Human Flea)

ball of pollen

Pollen-Carrying Leg (Worker Honeybee)

Brush foot

Middle foot

Food-Tasting Brush Foot (Butterfly)

**C. Abdomen:** This last section of the body contains the organs for digesting food, reproducing, and getting rid of waste products. The abdomen consists of 10–11 segments connected by flexible membranes. The segments can slide into one another like a telescope when the abdomen is empty or expand when it is full.

Some insects have a pair of feelers (*cerci*) on the last segment of the abdomen. The cerci on earwigs and some other insects form a pair of tongs which are used for self-defense or for capturing prey.

Many female insects have an egg-laying tool called the *ovipositor* in the last segments of the abdomen. It can be used to insert eggs into such things as soil, plants, or the bodies of other animals. Ovipositors of insects like bees and wasps have been adapted into a stinger.

# Is This an Insect? *(cont.)*

### *Inside Parts of Insects*

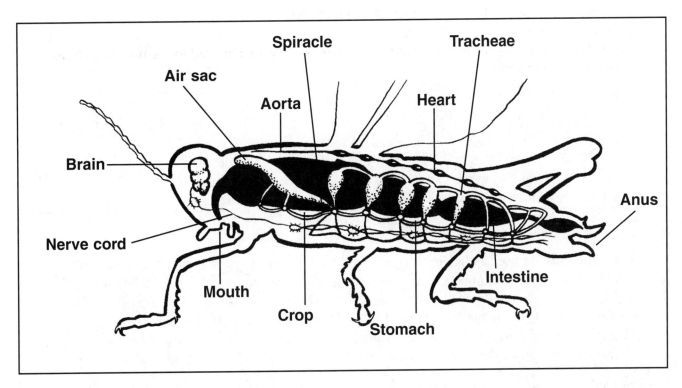

**Digestive System:** The digestive system of insects consists basically of a long tube that extends from the *mouth* to the anus. Food is chewed or sucked up by the mouthparts and then moves along the tube to the *crop* where it is stored and partly digested. The food later passes into the gizzard, which has muscular walls that contract and grind the food into small bits. Next, the food passes into the *stomach* where most digestion takes place. Nourishing parts of the food are absorbed into the blood, and wastes move into the *intestine*. Liquid and solid wastes are expelled through the *anus*.

**Respiratory System:** An insect breathes by means of tiny holes called *spiracles* along the sides of its body. Each hole leads into a large tube called a *trachea*. The large tubes divide into small tubes which also divide into still smaller tubes that branch out to all the cells of the body. This system of tubes carries oxygen to the cells and takes away carbon dioxide.

**Circulatory System:** An insect's blood does not flow through veins and arteries like ours. It fills the whole cavity of the insect's body and bathes all the organs and muscles. The blood circulates in a long tube just under the exoskeleton of the back. The pumping part of the tube, the *heart*, is in the abdomen. The front part of the tube extends into the head and is called the *aorta*. As the heart contracts, the blood is forced along the tube and out through the aorta. The blood first bathes the brain and then flows to other parts of the body. It then reenters the tube. An insect's blood is greenish, yellowish, or colorless.

**Nervous System:** This consists of a *brain* in the head and two *nerve cords* that lie side by side along the floor of the thorax and abdomen. The brain receives information from the eyes and antennae and controls the insect's body activities as a whole. Another nerve center in the head is connected to the brain and controls the insect's mouthparts.

# Mealworms

> ## Teacher Information
>
> Mealworms are not worms but the larval stage of a dark, flightless beetle. They are very clean, dry, and harmless to handle. It is easy to maintain mealworms in the classroom. They provide an excellent source for the study of the life cycle of an insect. They begin life inside a tiny egg, hatching as a larva within seven to ten days. The time spent in the larval stage varies. The larvae grow rapidly when the temperature is moderate and food is plentiful. They usually grow to about 25 mm in length and then become white pupae. The pupa is not rigid and will wiggle if touched, perhaps as a defense mechanism from predators. Legs and wings can be seen forming on the pupa through its thin skin, especially as it nears maturity. When the pupa begins to turn dark, it will soon become an adult. The adult begins laying eggs within two or three weeks after emerging from the pupal stage.
>
> Mealworms are used as fishing bait and food for a variety of pets, including lizards. It is best to purchase the jumbo size larvae so students can see more details. The larger-sized mealworms are usually available at bait stores. They are kept in the refrigerator to slow their growth while in the store but should be kept at room temperature in the classroom. These activities are designed to be conducted over many weeks, enabling students to observe and record the mealworms' physical changes during all stages of their lives.

**Overview:** *Students will investigate the characteristics and life cycle of mealworms.*

## Materials (for each student)

- jumbo-sized mealworms (available at pet stores or bait shops)
- blank 3" x 5" (8 cm x 13 cm) file cards
- two different colors of small sticky notes
- magnifier
- metric ruler

**Mealworm Care:** Since mealworms can eat through cardboard, use a plastic box to house them. Mealworms will eat dry grain such as oatmeal or bran, which may be used as both food and home for the larvae. Place 25–50 mealworms into the box and fill it with the grain to a depth of about 2.5" (6 cm). There is no need to put a lid on the box until beetles appear. You may want to place a piece of cheese cloth over the plastic box. Some moisture may be provided by putting a moist paper towel on top of the meal. The mealworms will nibble at the paper, which is not harmful to them. Replace the paper towel periodically and keep it moist. If the meal becomes moldy, too much moisture is being added.

# Mealworms *(cont.)*

## Activity 1

- Introduce the mealworm to the students so they will see that it is harmless and fragile, needing to be handled with care. You may want to place the mealworm in a small cup until the students feel at ease with handling it.

- Distribute a mealworm to each student and let each watch it for a while to observe how it moves. Monitor this study so none of the mealworms wanders off or falls off the tables. Encourage students who are reluctant to handle the larva to give it a name, making it a pet and less likely to arouse fear.

- After students have become familiar with their mealworms, issue each of them a magnifier and help them look closely at the physical characteristics of their larvae. They should notice that a larva has three pairs of legs with claw-like feet in front and four pairs toward the rear (false legs) with suction-cup feet. A single motionless leg is located at the very end of the larva. It has two short antennae, which help to identify the head. The eyes are not visible. The larva's body is divided into about 13 segments to enable it to be flexible, like our fingers.

- Lead a discussion of the observations students have made and then allow more time for observing the larvae. Encourage them to look closely for details of body parts and how larvae use their feet as they move.

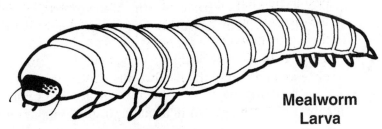

**Mealworm Larva**

## Activity 2

- Distribute mealworms and magnifiers to the students and let them observe the larvae again. Discuss what they have discovered about the mealworms thus far.

- Give each student a file card and have each draw his or her mealworms. (*Optional:* Draw the outline of the mealworm body and make copies on file cards for each student to fill in the details of features such as legs, segments, and antenna.) Be sure they write their names on the cards.

- Explain that these drawings are to be scientific, so no faces or shoes should appear. Monitor the students' progress and encourage them to use their magnifiers to look for details. You may want to display the drawings until they are needed for the next activity.

- Have students count the number of segments they see on their larvae. They may use the magnifiers to be sure their count is as accurate as possible. Give each student a self-adhesive note. Have each one write his or her name on it as well as the number of segments counted.

- Ask for the number of segments students counted. Write the number of segments reported below a horizontal line drawn on large paper. Have students put their sticky notes in a vertical row above the number, without overlapping them. Draw a vertical line to the left side of the notes, beginning at the horizontal line. Divide this line with numbered marks to indicate the number of self-adhesive sticky notes. The data on the notes will form a bar graph.

# Mealworms *(cont.)*

## Activity 2 *(cont.)*

- Help students determine the average number of segments by looking at the graph. If any count is more than two segments above or below the average, have those students recount their larva's segments with the assistance of another student.

## Activity 3

- Distribute the mealworms and the drawings made in Activity 1. It is not necessary for students to have the same mealworms as they had in the previous activity.

- Give students metric rulers. Tell them they are to measure the length of their mealworms. Let the students use their problem-solving skills to determine how this can be done. Have them record the length on the file card by drawing a line the length they measured and writing the length to the nearest millimeter.

- Distribute a sticky note to each student and on it have each record his or her name as well as the length of the mealworm. Create a bar graph with the resulting data on another piece of large paper. Discuss the various lengths of mealworms. Have students remeasure any which are doubtful. Let them determine the average size of their mealworms.

## Activity 4

- Let each student have his or her own mealworm to observe for the next two or three weeks. Each mealworm can be placed in a small plastic container with a lid. Poke holes in the lid to permit an air flow.

- Have students maintain a record on file cards, including dates, measurements, and careful drawings. Be sure they add color when they draw the beetle.

- Tell students to use their data to calculate the time elapsed between the mealworm as a larva and when it becomes a pupa, as well as the time elapsing from pupal stage to adult. This data can be graphed to determine the average time in each cycle for the students' mealworms.

**Mealworm Beetle**

## Closure

- Display the graphs and student drawings.

- When the study ends, let the students make a booklet of their file cards, adding a cover of their own design.

*Note:* Since mealworms serve as pet food, a student with a lizard, land turtle, or other pet may be able to get permission from home to take the mealworm culture at the end of this study.

# Ants

### Teacher Information

There are over 2,500 species of ants, all social animals which live and work together in colonies. They are the most familiar of insects and have often been compared to human societies. Each ant in a colony has specific duties. A single *queen* ant reproduces all of the colony's members. She may live as long as 20 years. The *male* ant is responsible for mating with the queen. This occurs outside the colony when the queen and males develop wings. After mating, the males die and the queen tears off her wings and returns to her nest as an additional queen or begins her own nest. The *soldier* ants are responsible for protecting the members of the colony. The *worker* ants are all female and are responsible for the maintenance of the colony. Their jobs may range from husking seeds and carrying out dirt to digging new tunnels and feeding the larvae. An ant colony consists of many (sometimes millions) of ants working cooperatively to form a single society.

## Carpenter Ants in a Colony

**queen**

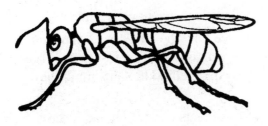

**male**

**worker** (normal size)

**soldier**

# Ants *(cont.)*

## *Ants in the Wild*

**Overview:** *Students observe and collect data about ants in the wild.*

## Materials

- 3" x 5" (8 cm x 13 cm) file cards
- Observing Ants in the Wild Data Sheet (page 17)
- *optional:* magnifier for each student

## Lesson Preparation

- Find a source of wild ants near school for students to observe. Watch how they behave and try the various experiments which will be conducted with the students in this lesson.
- During observations of the ants, you may consider having students use a piece of newspaper to sit on. This will help those somewhat frightened by insects to feel more secure than just sitting on the ground.
- Consider taking photographs of all students observing ants during this study. The photos can be included in the book they will be making of their data sheets.

## Activity

1. Distribute a file card to each student and have each draw an ant from memory. It should be as large as the file card to show details. Tell students they will study ants for many weeks, beginning by watching ants near school to see how they behave.

2. Take the students to an area near school to observe ants in the wild. Have them watch ants moving, asking them to describe the movement. (*Usually ants move in a line, following a scent trail laid down by the earlier ants.*)

3. Conduct some simple experiments with the ants so students can see how they react.
   - Draw a line through the line of ants so students can see how the ants react. (*The ants will become disoriented for a while but then find their way again.*) Let them watch to see how the ants reestablish the new trail. Ask students to think what method the ants might have used to find their path again.
   - Place an obstacle (e.g., pebble) in the line of ants so students can watch and discuss their reaction. (*They may go around it or climb over it.*) See if they can guess why the ants behave in the manner they do.
   - Put food (pieces of meat, candy, seeds, sugar cereal) in the ants' path and observe how they react. If they carry off the food, point out how much larger the pieces are than the ants. Have students notice that ants use their mouths to hold the food.
   - Let the students think of ways to study the ants and carry out their experiments.

4. Follow the ants' trail to find where it begins and ends.

## Closure

- Return to the classroom and group the students. Distribute the data sheets to the students and have them write illustrated stories about their observations of ants in the wild.
- Collect the drawings to keep for an ant book students will assemble at the end of their study.

# Ants _(cont.)_

## *Observing Ants in the Wild Data Sheet*

**To the Student:** Draw pictures about six different things you learned as you watched the ants in the wild. Write a sentence about the picture in each of the boxes below your picture.

| | |
|---|---|
| **1**<br><br><br><br>_____<br>_____ | **2**<br><br><br><br>_____<br>_____ |
| **3**<br><br><br><br>_____<br>_____ | **4**<br><br><br><br>_____<br>_____ |
| **5**<br><br><br><br>_____<br>_____ | **6**<br><br><br><br>_____<br>_____ |

# Ants (cont.)

## *Ant Farming*

**Overview:** *Students will make observations of ants being placed in a commercial habitat.*

## Materials

- one or two commercial ant farms (See resources.)
- magnifiers for each student
- Ants in an Ant Farm Data Sheet (page 19)
- *optional:* video camera

## Lesson Preparation

- Order the ant farm(s) early enough to allow time to send in the coupon for the live specimens. Assemble the ant farm(s) but do not add the ants. Label the sides of the ant habitats A and B for observations.

- You may want to record the assembling of the ant farm(s) on video, as well as the ants' first reaction to being inside it. This can be the introduction of a video record which is made throughout the raising of the ants.

## Activity

1. Remind the students of their observations of ants in the wild. Explain that the ants live under the ground, and it is impossible to watch them there. Let them know that you are going to prepare a special home for some ants that will let them observe what their homes look like.

2. Gather the students near the ant farm(s) and let them observe as you put the material into the habitat(s). Follow the directions to introduce the ants into the ant farm(s). Let students observe what the ants do as they enter their new home. Encourage them to look for details.

3. Distribute the Ants in an Ant Farm Data Sheet to each of them. Tell the students to draw the details of what they observed as the ants' nest was being prepared and how the ants reacted when they were released into it.

## Closure

- Have the students share their drawings with others in the class.
- Collect the drawings for the students' ant book.

# Ants *(cont.)*

## *Ants in an Ant Farm Data Sheet*

**To the Student:** Draw pictures about six different things you saw happen as you watched the farm being filled and what the ants did when they were put into their new home. Write a sentence about the picture in each of the boxes below.

| 1 | 2 |
|---|---|
| 3 | 4 |
| 5 | 6 |

# Ants *(cont.)*

## *Ants Up Close*

**Overview:** *Students will make observations of ants in captivity.*

## Materials

- ant farm(s) prepared in previous lesson
- colored pens or colored pencils
- *optional:* video camera and tripod
- Ant Farm Observations Data Sheet (page 21)
- magnifiers

## Lesson Preparation

- Set the ant farm(s) at work station(s) in the room, away from direct sunlight.

- Design a schedule for small groups of students to observe the ant farms daily for at least 10 minutes.

- Decide on the color to be used each day for showing the new tunnel additions.

- A video camera may be used to make a scientific record of the changes in the ant farm(s). The recording can be done as time-lapse photography. This will require that a few seconds of video be taken each day of the same side of one ant farm and from the same location. The zoom lens can be used to take closeups of the ants at work. Mark the placement of the ant farm on the table and the location of the camera so they will be the same during the daily recordings. When played back, the view of the ants working will be speeded up to show this in a few minutes rather than many days. Students can then make more detailed observations, just as scientists do.

## Activity

1. Discuss what the students saw as the ant farm(s) was assembled in the previous lesson. If available, show the video made during that lesson.

2. Distribute a data sheet to each student and explain how they will work in groups to observe the ants each day. Review the information on the data sheet so they will see that they are to make pencil drawings on their data sheets of the tunnels the ants made and then color them with the color you designate for that day. They will use a new color to continue the recording the next day, beginning where the tunnel left off the previous day. In this way, the new additions to the tunnel will be obvious.

3. Have the students continue to make daily records of the ant farm for at least two weeks.

## Closure

- After the ants have formed many tunnels, cover one side of the habitat with black paper. Let students continue to record the uncovered side for about a week and then remove the paper.

- Have students compare the differences between sides. (*They should see many more tunnels on the side which was covered.*) Tell them to discuss why they think this happened. (*Ants live underground where it is dark. When the ant farm is covered, it was much more like their natural habitat.*)

# Ants (cont.)

## Ant Farm Observations Data Sheet

Name:_____ Date:_____

**To the Student:** Observe the ant farm for at least two weeks, making drawings to show the changes you see. Add the changes in the tunnels to the last drawings in pencil and then trace over them with colored pen or pencil. Use a different color each day and record that day's color on the key by coloring the circle beside the date. If there is no change, record the data and write "no change" in the color column. Record both sides of the ant farm each day.

### Key

Date                                Color

_____           ○

_____           ○

_____           ○

_____           ○

_____           ○

_____           ○

_____           ○

### Ant Farm Side A

A

### Key

Date                                Color

_____           ○

_____           ○

_____           ○

_____           ○

_____           ○

_____           ○

_____           ○

### Ant Farm Side B

B

Make notes of interesting things you see happen. Be sure to include the dates of these observations. If you need more space for your notes, use another piece of lined paper.

# Ants *(cont.)*

## *Ant Book*

**Overview:** *Students will create a book from their ant data sheets.*

## Materials

- ant data sheets and drawings from previous lessons
- large construction paper or file folders
- crayons or colored pens
- transparency and copies of Body Parts of an Ant (page 23)

## Activity

1. Let the students discuss some of the things they have learned about ants in this study. If available, show the video record of the ant. Discuss it as it is being viewed to point out the details of body structure and ant behavior.

2. Show the transparency of Body Parts of an Ant and discuss its details, as appropriate for this class.

3. Tell the students that they are going to create a science book from all the data sheets they have been doing during this study. Explain that this is just what real scientists do with their records.

4. Distribute large construction paper or file folders and crayons or pens. Tell the students to design a cover for their book which will show what they have learned about ants. Encourage them to be creative.

## Closure

- Let students draw a picture on the inside of their book cover to show what they may have looked like to the ants they were studying. Remind them that the ants, like most insects, only see things which are close to them. Thus, they would see details of their faces only. Provide mirrors for the students to look at themselves as they do their drawings or have them draw each other.

- Have the students place their file card drawings and data sheets inside their covers. Distribute a copy of the Body Parts of an Ant for them to include in their book. If photographs of the students were taken during this study, distribute them to be enclosed in their book.

### *Body Parts of an Ant*

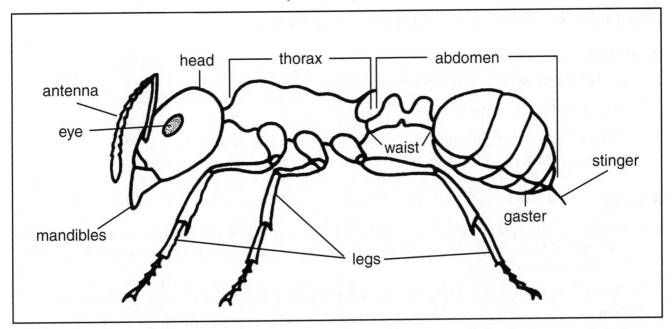

An ant is an insect and therefore has three main body parts—(1) the *head*, (2) the *thorax*, and (3) the *abdomen*. The main features of the head are the *eyes*, *antennae*, and *mandibles* (jaws). Three pairs of legs are attached to the thorax. The narrow front part of the abdomen is called the *waist*. Some ants have a *stinger* at the tip of the abdomen.

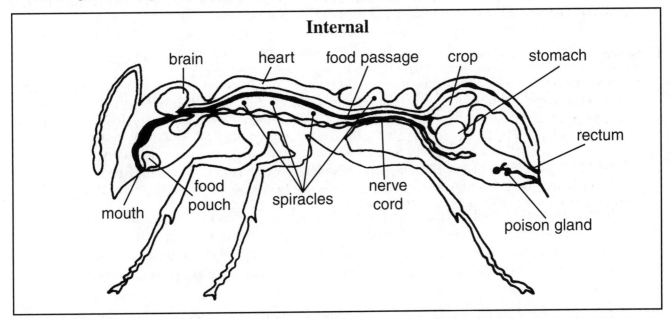

An ant's internal organs include a *brain* and *nerve cord* and a tube-like *heart*. The ant breathes through *spiracles*, which are tiny openings along the sides of its body. Its digestive system includes a food pouch that squeezes the liquid out of food. The liquid moves through a food passage to the *crop*, a storage pouch, and then to the *stomach*, where digestion occurs. Wastes pass through the *rectum* and out of the body. Only ants with stingers have the poison glands at the top of the abdomen.

# Butterflies

## Teacher Information

Butterflies are found nearly everywhere in the world. One of the most common of these is the painted lady butterfly, which will be used in this study. In the wild these butterflies are not harmful to commercial crops since they eat the mallow (malva) or hollyhock leaves, which are weeds.

The larva hatches from a tiny, pale green egg and then begins to feed. As the larva grows, it sheds its tight skin (a process called *molting*) and leaves it in a black furry ball. About 10 days after hatching, the larva hangs upside down and prepares to become a *pupa*. After 24 hours, the caterpillar's skin splits, and the thin brown *chrysalis* which has formed under the skin encases the pupa and will harden in about four hours. Butterfly pupae are enclosed in a chrysalis, not a cocoon. The pupae of most moths are encased in a *cocoon* made of silken thread produced by the moth larva and woven around its body.

The adult butterfly emerges in 7 to 10 days and expands its wings with fluid pumped from its abdomen. The wings take about an hour to harden before the butterfly can take flight. Some red fluid may be expelled, a waste material accumulated during the pupal stage.

Painted lady butterflies are easy to raise. The larvae and food are available commercially. (See page 48.) Small plastic vials with lids are supplied, one for each larva. The food, in the form of a paste, is sent with the larva and is divided among the vials. The larvae are placed inside, and then the vials are capped. The containers are kept in a well-lighted area where the temperature is 75°–80° F (24°–27° C). Each larva will form its chrysalis on the lid of its vial as it enters the pupa stage. The pupa is then transferred into an enclosure where the adult will eventually emerge.

When the adult butterfly first emerges, its long tube-like mouth (*proboscis*) is in two parts. The butterfly extends the pieces of the proboscis several times until the parts are joined lengthwise into one hollow tube. It curls up outside the head when not in use. The butterfly will drink nectar through this straw-like mouth in the wild. In captivity, it can drink juice from pieces of fruit such as orange or watermelon. These may be placed on the bottom of the butterfly enclosure and replaced every two days.

Butterflies will mate after emerging, and the females may begin to lay eggs within five to seven days after they emerge. The eggs will hatch in three to five days. It is best to free the butterflies within three days of their emerging so the eggs can be laid in the wild. Release the butterfly on a sunny day in an area where there are plants, preferably weeds.

The release is a great event, and all students should participate. If they sit or stand very still as the butterflies are released, they may be treated to having a butterfly land on them. It is as if the butterflies are bidding their "parents" farewell before flying off to make their own way in the world. Students may see the butterflies in the area for several days after the release.

# Butterflies *(cont.)*

## *Recording Larvae Growth*

**Overview:** *Students will observe and record the growth of larvae until they become pupae.* (Note: This activity and the next will require approximately five to nine days from the day the painted lady larvae arrive.)

## Materials

- 30 live painted lady butterfly larvae (Purchase from Insect Lore; see Resources section.)
- vials with lids and food (included with butterfly larvae)
- two paper towels
- copies of Painted Lady Butterfly Larvae Record (page 26)
- metric ruler
- magnifier

## Lesson Preparation

- Use the lid from one of the vials to draw 30 circles on the paper towel. Cut out the circles to be placed inside the lid. Use a pencil and label each paper circle (1–30).
- Distribute nutrient into the vials and carefully transfer one larva into each. Put the paper circle (number should be visible through the vial) and then lid over the top of each container.
- If there are no holes in the lids, use a pin to poke about five holes in each.
- Use a permanent felt pen and label each lid with the same number as the paper inside the lid.

## Activity

1. Ask the students how many have seen butterflies. Let them describe these to the class. Tell the students that they are going to raise painted lady butterflies from the larva stage.
2. Distribute a magnifier and larva to each student. Caution them to keep vial lids closed to avoid letting germs enter. Explain that they should not shake or drop the container or the larva will become frightened. Tell them to examine the larva with their magnifiers and discuss the details with a partner. (*Some may see green balls on the food; these are feces from the larva.*)
3. Distribute a record sheet to each student and have each put his or her name and vial number on it. Show them how to write today's date below the first vial.
4. Help them measure the larva through the container, gently turning it on its side if necessary.
5. Have students draw their larva, using a magnifier to view the details of legs, feet, and head. The drawings should be life-size and show the larva's location inside the vial.

## Closure

- Students will keep daily records of their larva until it becomes a pupa.
- Have them compare the growth of their larva with those of other students in the class. Let them calculate and record the difference between each day's growth.
- Save all records students make to enclose in a butterfly book at the end of this study.
- *Optional:* Make a time-lapse video of one larva's growth to adulthood so students can replay it at the end of the study.
- *Optional:* Take photographs of the students and their butterflies at different stages to include in their butterfly book.

# **Butterflies** *(cont.)*

## *Painted Lady Butterfly Larvae Record*

Student Name: _____ Vial # _____

**To the Student:** Measure and record your butterfly larva each day without removing the lid of the vial.

Date: _____

Length: _____mm

Date: _____

Length: _____mm

Growth: _____mm

Date: _____

Length: _____mm

Growth: _____mm

Date: _____

Length: _____mm

Growth: _____mm

Date: _____

Length: _____mm

Growth: _____mm

Date: _____

Length: _____mm

Growth: _____mm

Date: _____

Length: _____mm

Growth: _____mm

Date: _____

Length: _____mm

Growth: _____mm

Date: _____

Length: _____mm

Growth: _____mm

# Butterflies *(cont.)*

## *Getting to Know Your Larva*

Student Name: _____ Vial #_____

**To the Student:** Use your magnifier to see the details of your painted lady larva and complete the information below.

1. Look at the bristles which are called setae *(sē tē)* on the caterpillar (larva).

   • What color are they? _____

   • Are there little setae coming out of the bigger ones? _____

   • Draw a large picture of one seta in the circle.

2. Why do you think the larva has setae?_____

   _____

3. Look at the legs of your larva. How many does it have? _____

4. Are the legs exactly alike? _____

   • Draw the legs on the right places on the larva outline below.

## Painted Lady Butterfly Larva

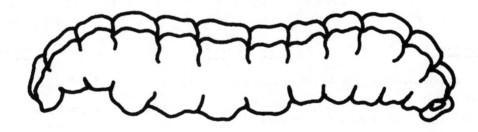

5. Draw the mouthparts of the larva below. Use your magnifier to make this picture large enough to show the details.

## Larva Mouthparts

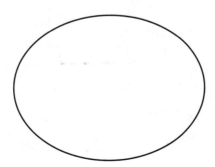

# Butterflies (cont.)

### *How Does Your Larva Grow?*

**Overview:** *Students will graph and analyze the growth data of the painted lady larvae.*

## Materials

- Painted Lady Butterfly Larvae Record (from previous activity)
- transparency and copies of Graphing Larva Growth (page 29)

## Lesson Preparation

Wait until the larvae have all become pupa to do this activity.

## Activity

1. Discuss what students have learned about the larvae up until this point. Be sure they know that the black "fuzzy" balls are not feces but the skin which is shed by the larvae as they become too big for it. It is important for students to notice that not all larvae become pupa at the same time, even though they were all the same age when first being measured. Just like other animals, including humans, growth varies with each individual.

2. Let students examine the pupa and make a final drawing of it on their record sheet.

3. Distribute a copy of Graphing Larvae Growth to each student and go over the instructions. Use the transparency to show how to place dates on the graph. Show them how to plot the first data from record sheets, showing the larva length in millimeters when they began measuring. Let them add the rest of the data, and then show them how to connect the data points as a line graph.

4. Compare the differences in the lengths of the various larvae. Like the students, even though the larvae are all about the same age, their sizes are different.

## Closure

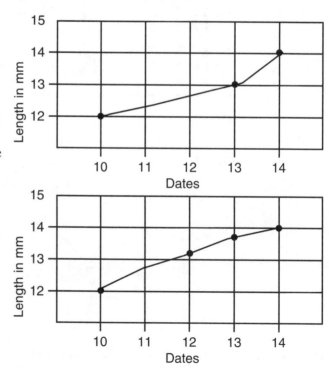

- Help students complete the graph summary by filling in the missing information. This can be done by following the line between the data points on either side of the missing data and seeing where it crosses the line for the missing date(s). As in the example, data for the 11th and 12th were not plotted. The line joining the data for the 10th and 13th shows the length on these dates was approximately 12.5 mm and 12.7 mm, respectively.

- Explain how they can tell when their larva grew most rapidly. (*The graph line will rise rapidly.*) In the example shown here, the fastest growth was between the 10th and 12th.

- See if all the larvae had their fastest growth at the same time. (*This is not very likely to happen.*)

# Butterflies *(cont.)*

## *Graphing Larva Growth*

Student Name: _____ Vial #_____

**To the Student:** Make a graph using the data you collected on the Painted Lady Butterfly Larva Record. Write the dates for this study along the bottom of the graph, including weekends and holidays. Plot the data on the graph. Connect the dots when all data has been entered.

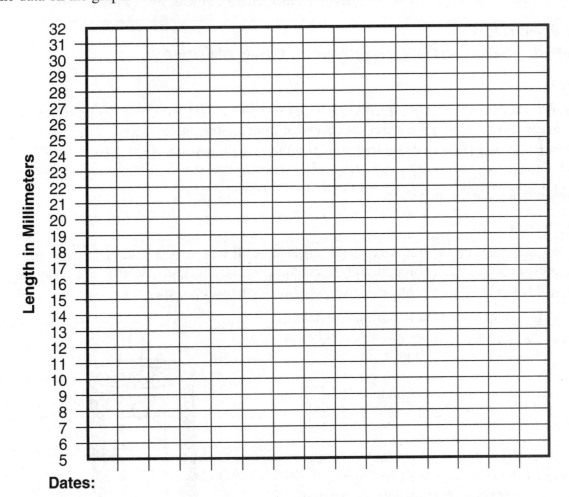

**Dates:**

## Graph Summary

List the dates when you did not measure the larva. Use your graph to find this missing data and record it.

**Date**                    **Larva Size from Graph**

_____          _____ mm

_____          _____ mm

_____          _____ mm

Use the graph to find between which dates your larva grew most rapidly: _____ and _____

# Butterflies (cont.)

## *Chrysalis to Butterfly*

### Teacher Information

Once the larva has formed a chrysalis, it should be carefully transferred to a butterfly enclosure. Students will draw their chrysalides and keep a record of them throughout the period of their development. Hopefully, they will witness the emergence of at least one of the butterflies.

**Overview:** *Students will watch the transformation of pupa to adult butterfly.*

## Materials

- two pairs of 12-inch (30 cm) embroidery hoops (available at most stores which carry yarn)
- 1.5 yards (1.4 m) netting 45-inch (114 cm) wide from a fabric store
- 12-inch diameter circle of cardboard (laminated to make it reusable)
- Chrysalis to Butterfly Record (page 32)
- The Butterfly's Story (page 34)

## Lesson Preparation

Follow the instructions below to make butterfly enclosures. It will be best if several are made to spread the pupae out and make it easier for students to continue their study. Each butterfly enclosure will look like a tube of net gathered at the top and bottom and held open at each end by the embroidery hoops.

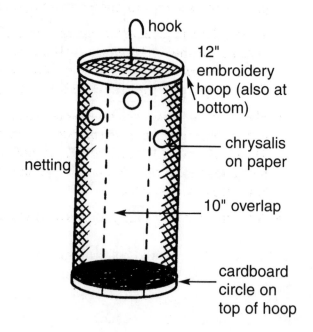

- Work on a large table with an assistant to help you. Lay the netting flat on the table and fold it lengthwise so it forms a 10-inch (25 cm) overlap.
- Tie heavy string or yarn around the netting about 6 inches (15 cm) from each end to form the tube.
- Insert the inner hoop from one pair of hoops inside the net tube as close to the top as possible.
- Place the outer hoop over this one on the outside of the net tube to secure the hoop to the net.
- Place the other hoop at the bottom of the tube.
- Use a large paper clip to make the hook and suspend the tube from the ceiling.
- Have someone else hold the net tube up while you adjust the hoops so the tube hangs straight.
- Place the cardboard circle inside the net tube at the bottom where it can rest on the hoop.
- Remove the chrysalis (pupa) from the vial, being careful not to dislodge it from the paper. Pin the paper to the inside of the net tube, keeping the chrysalis facing away from the net. Use toothpicks to keep the overlap area closed to prevent the butterflies from escaping.

# Butterflies *(cont.)*

### *Chrysalis to Butterfly (cont.)*

## Activity

1. Let the students find their butterfly chrysalis by the number on the paper to which it is attached. (If a pupa has become dislodged from the paper, just lay it on the bottom of the tube on top of the paper so the number can identify it. It should be able to emerge.)

2. Tell the students that the larva is undergoing a great many changes during this stage of its life. Distribute a copy of the Chrysalis to Butterfly Record and explain that they should draw the chrysalis in the box. Tell them to draw what they think the larva will become when it emerges beside the drawing of the chrysalis.

3. Help students complete their pictures using colors that match those of the chrysalides.

4. Over the next few days, have students watch their pupae carefully to look for colors of wings showing through. See if they can find which end is the head and alert them to look for legs. The chrysalides should not be removed or handled during this time.

5. The butterfly should begin to emerge about 7–10 days after it becomes a pupa. (*Note:* The butterfly "emerges" from the chrysalis; it does not "hatch" as it does from the egg.)

## Closure

- Read the painted lady butterfly information (page 24) regarding what to look for during emergence and be ready to share this with the students as the pupae begin to darken. This will prepare the students to make careful observations of those which emerge during class time.

- When a butterfly begins to emerge, have all the students gather to watch the process. They should watch as the butterfly pumps fluid into its wings and extends and curls its tongue to glue the two halves together. If red fluid is excreted, remind them that this is normal. The butterfly is getting rid of wastes that formed while it was a pupa.

- Place cut fruit (e.g., watermelon or oranges) on the bottom of the enclosure. The butterflies will gather there, and students can observe them use their long tube-like mouths to drink the juice. They can survive for several days inside the butterfly enclosure but should be released when all pupae have emerged. Follow the teacher information (page 24) for more details on how the butterflies may be released.

- After the butterflies are released, distribute a copy of The Butterfly's Story to each student.

# Butterflies (cont.)

### Chrysalis to Butterfly Record

Student Name: _____ Vial #_____

**To the Student:** Use a magnifier to look carefully at your chrysalis. Make a large drawing of the chrysalis below. Draw the antennae, eyes, wings, legs, and abdomen, which you can see through the skin of the chrysalis. Be sure to label these parts on your drawing.

**Painted Lady Chrysalis**

• Carefully color the chrysalis as close to its real colors as possible.

• When the chrysalis is about seven days old, it will turn dark. What do you suppose this means?

_____

• When the chrysalis turns dark, look for the wings and see if you can detect the colors of the wings through the thin shell. What colors do you see? _____

• What is the date you first began your observations of the larva? _____

• When did the chrysalis become a butterfly? _____

• From the larva stage, how many days did it take the larva to become a butterfly? _____

• Draw a picture of your beautiful butterfly below.

**My Painted Lady Butterfly**

# Butterflies *(cont.)*

## *The Butterfly's Story*

**Overview:** *Students will culminate their study of butterflies by writing the life story of a butterfly and making a butterfly book using their data sheets.*

## Materials

- butterfly record sheets made in previous lessons
- large construction paper
- copies of The Butterfly's Story (page 34)
- colored pens or crayons
- *optional:* colored tissue

## Activity

1. Review all that students have learned about butterflies as they observed the painted lady butterflies. If available, show the time-lapse video record of this.

2. Tell the students that they are going to make a butterfly book that will be like a scientist's notebook since it will have all the records they made of their butterflies.

3. Distribute a copy of The Butterfly's Story and review the instructions with the students. Tell them this will be the last page they place in their butterfly book. Encourage them to use their data sheets as they write the story and complete the life cycle chart.

## Closure

- Distribute construction paper to the students and have them create a cover for their butterfly book. They could make a butterfly on the cover using torn pieces of brightly colored tissue paper.

- Have students make their butterfly book enclosing their data sheets and The Butterfly's Story, as well as any photographs taken of butterflies during their study.

# Butterflies (cont.)

## *The Butterfly's Story* (cont.)

Student Name: _____

**To the Student:** Pretend you are a butterfly talking to a butterfly larva. Tell the larva how it will change as it grows up. Make drawings inside the circles of what the larva will look like as it changes.

Hello, little larva. Someday you will be a beautiful butterfly just like me. Let me tell you how you are going to change into a butterfly.

First, you will _____

_____

_____.

You will look like this:

Since you get too big for your skin, you will

_____.

The old skin looks like this:

Finally, you will hang _____.

You will look like this:

Now it is time for you to _____

_____.

You will look like this:

At last you will _____

and become a _____.

You will look like this:

# Silkworms

## Teacher Information

Raising silkworms (*sericulture*) is one of man's oldest occupations, beginning in China nearly 5,000 years ago. The silk spun by a silkworm in making its cocoon is woven into the most beautiful fabric in the world, at one time used only for royalty in China. Possession of silkworms was a closely guarded secret by the Chinese for several thousand years. Not until the 11th century did European traders manage to steal a few eggs and carry them to Europe to begin silkworm rearing. Sericulture spread rapidly throughout Europe and Asia during the following centuries.

Silkworm eggs are available commercially. It is important to order the eggs in the spring when mulberry trees begin to produce leaves, for these are the silkworm's only source of food. The tiny eggs may be placed in the bottom of a small cardboard box. Before hatching, the eggs will turn darker around the edges. When the tiny worms hatch, they will be about the size of a comma. They should be picked up with a small paintbrush and placed on a clean, fresh young mulberry leaf.

During the first week, fresh leaves should be placed on top of old ones which contain the larvae. After the first week, the larvae will be large enough to eat the leaves before they dry out, and you will need only to lay clean fresh leaves over them. Sometime during each day remove old or bare leaves from the rearing box. Silkworms have become so domesticated through thousands of years that they depend completely on humans to care for them. To clean the leaves, rinse and drain them before using. Leaves may be stored in the refrigerator in a plastic bag.

The larvae molt about four times as they outgrow their skins. After 25–30 days the silkworms will stop eating. Soon after this, they begin to rear their heads and move them back and forth above the rest of the body. The larvae become slightly smaller and may have a slight color change. The silkworm begins to look for a quiet corner to form its cocoon. It builds the wall of the cocoon by making rows and rows of two continuous strands of silk. It produces the silk in two special glands and sends it out a tube called a *spinneret*, located near its lower lip. The silk comes out a liquid but quickly dries in the air. After the cocoon is done, the silkworm sheds its skin, and the pupa wiggles free, encased inside the cocoon. Within the pupa, the new silk moth begins to form.

The moth escapes from the cocoon by producing a fluid from the mouth that dissolves a hole through the silk. When the hole is big enough, the moth slips through. This usually takes place early in the morning. The moth will fill its tiny wings with fluid. These are far too small for it to fly away. Mating begins almost immediately and may last about a day. Egg laying begins as soon as pairs separate. These are laid in neat rows upon any surface. Egg laying may continue for about a week, most eggs being laid on the first three days. Females may lay about 500 yellow eggs, which later turn grey. The eggs must be refrigerated (not frozen) until the next spring before they will hatch. When the leaves return in the spring, the cycle can begin again.

# Silkworms (cont.)

### Silkworm Larvae

**Overview:** *Students will raise silkworm larvae and record growth.*

## Materials

- 25 silkworm eggs (See Carolina Biological resource on page 48.)
- mulberry leaves (required as food)
- silk cloth (e.g., scarf) and polyester cloth
- cardboard boxes (Gift boxes will do.)
- Silkworm Growth Record (page 38)

- magnifier and metric ruler for each student
- transparency of Life Cycle of the Silkworm Moth (page 37)
- snack-sized resealable bag
- *optional:* microscope
- *optional:* video camera

## Lesson Preparation

- Order silkworm eggs to arrive when mulberry leaves are available.
- Usually eggs arrive glued to paper, just as they were laid. Snip off a tiny piece of the paper with 1–3 eggs attached and place it in a zip-lock bag.
- After the larvae hatch, divide them into several small, shallow cardboard boxes.

## Activity

1. Let students feel the silk and polyester cloth. Explain that the polyester cloth is made from petroleum. Tell them that the silk is made by the caterpillar (*larva*) of a special moth. Let them know that they are going to raise the larvae of the silk moth so they can see this fabric being spun.

2. Divide students into small groups and provide each with a magnifier and a bag with silkworm eggs. Let students see the eggs through a microscope if available. Tell them the bag will keep the eggs clean and safe and should therefore not be opened.

3. Give each student a copy of the Silkworm Growth Record and help them complete their first drawing of the egg. The records should be collected after each class and returned to the students after the eggs hatch so students can add more information.

4. Show the Life Cycle of the Silkworm Moth transparency so students can see about how long it will take to witness the entire cycle.

5. After eggs hatch and the larvae are divided into separate boxes, divide students into small groups and assign each to watch a different box. Have students use the magnifiers (and microscope) to make their records. Help students measure the tiny silkworm and record its length. You may need to make more copies of the record sheet for students since the larvae take so long to grow.

## Closure

- When silkworms are large enough to pick up, place them on pieces of mulberry leaf. Give one to each student to watch it as it eats the leaf. Have them make drawings of their silkworms eating and write descriptions of what they see, hear, and feel. Save this and the other record sheet(s) for their silkworm book.

- If possible, make a video record of the growth of the silkworms in time-lapse, about 30 seconds of video each time to show the larva's growth and complete life cycle.

# Silkworms *(cont.)*

*Life Cycle of the Silkworm Moth*

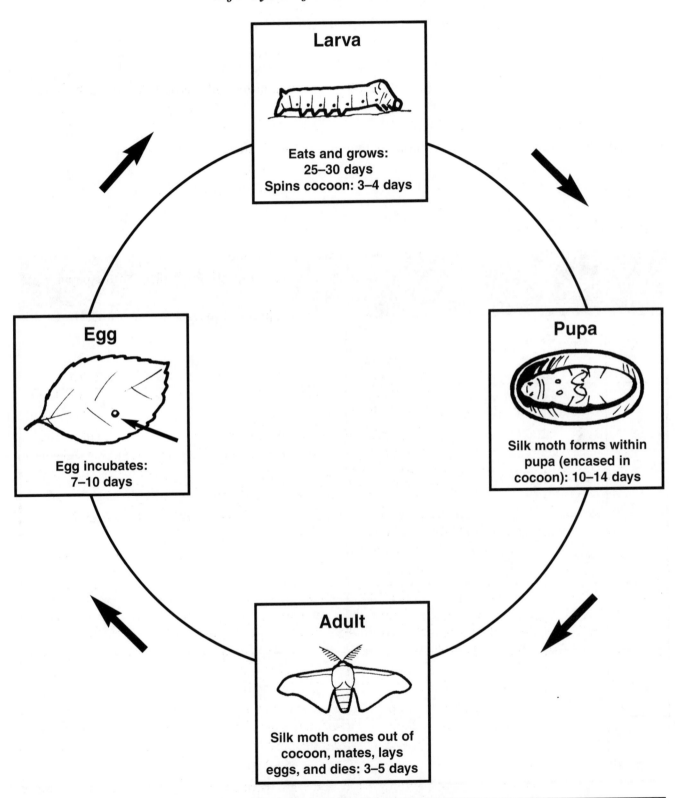

**Larva**

Eats and grows:
25–30 days
Spins cocoon: 3–4 days

**Egg**

Egg incubates:
7–10 days

**Pupa**

Silk moth forms within
pupa (encased in
cocoon): 10–14 days

**Adult**

Silk moth comes out of
cocoon, mates, lays
eggs, and dies: 3–5 days

**Total Life Cycle: 48–63 days**

# Silkworms *(cont.)*

### *Silkworm Growth Record*

Student Name: _____ Date Study Began: _____

**To the Student:** Keep a record of the silkworm so you can find out how it grows and changes.

Show what a silkworm egg looks like through a magnifier.

After the egg hatches, use a magnifier to help you see the tiny larva. Measure it and record the date and size on the chart. Finally, make a drawing of the silkworm.

| Date | Size | Picture | Date | Size | Picture |
|------|------|---------|------|------|---------|
|  |  |  |  |  |  |
|  |  |  |  |  |  |
|  |  |  |  |  |  |
|  |  |  |  |  |  |
|  |  |  |  |  |  |
|  |  |  |  |  |  |
|  |  |  |  |  |  |

On the back of this paper, tell some of the things you have learned about your silkworm during this study.

# Silkworms *(cont.)*

### *Larva to Pupa*

**Overview:** *Students will observe the pupa stage of the silkworm moth and unwind the silk from several cocoons.*

## Materials

- silkworm larvae (entering or at pupa stage)
- egg cartons
- copies of the Silkworm Growth Record from previous lesson
- Life Cycle of the Silkworm Moth Data Sheet (page 41)
- hot water
- empty spools
- mugs or cups

## Lesson Preparation

- Transfer the pupae to the egg cartons as they are forming their cocoon or after they are formed. The remaining larvae may continue to be fed and kept in their boxes. Place the cocoons in separate egg boxes so they will continue to be observed by the same groups of students.

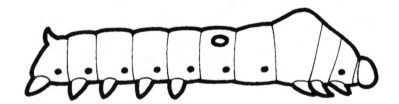

**Larva**

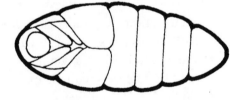

**Pupa**

- When some of the larvae have entered the pupa stage and their cocoons are completed, select one from each group plus one more. These will be killed so the silk can be taken from the cocoon. If the adult moth emerges, the silk thread is broken and will not unwind as one thread. The extra cocoon will be opened to show students the pupa inside, which is different from the larva. To kill the pupa, bake the cocoons in an oven at about 200°F for 30 minutes.

- To prepare the cocoons for unwinding, place them in boiling water and boil them for about five minutes, turning them over and over with a fork. The silk will begin to loosen, and some tangled threads will appear around each of the cocoons. Remove them with a fork and place each in a cup of hot water. Find the end of the strand with your fingers by dipping the cocoon up and down in the water until you find a single strand of silk that pulls away easily. Put the end of that strand over the empty spool and begin to unwind it onto the spool. One large cocoon may have half a mile of unbroken thread. The dead pupa will be found after all the thread is unwound.

# Silkworms (cont.)

## Larva to Pupa (cont.)

## Activity

1. Review the Silkworm Growth Records with the students to summarize what they have learned to this point about the silkworm larvae. Have students add new information to the record.

2. Distribute a copy of the Life Cycle of the Silkworm Moth Data Sheet and have students complete the data which have been gathered thus far.

3. Compare their data with that on the same chart used at the beginning of this study. Discuss the differences in the length of time their silkworms went through their stages and those shown on the other chart. Have the various groups compare their data as well.

4. After the cocoons are about five days old, select those to be used for gathering the silk threads and one to be opened to show the pupa inside. Follow the instructions in the Lesson Preparation section to start the process of unwinding the cocoon.

5. Assign stations for students to work in and wind the silk on to the spool of thread. Keep the water in the cup to help the cocoon remain soft. It should be replaced with clean, warm water periodically. This process may take some time, for a large cocoon may have as much as ¹/₂ mile (.8 km) of silk in it.

6. Use cuticle scissors to cut open the extra cocoon and let the students see its contents. Find the last skin shed by the larva within the cocoon. Discuss how the pupa is different from the larva. Let students use magnifiers to examine the pupa and see if they can find the legs and segmented body. When the silk is unwound from the cocoons, have them examine those pupae as well.

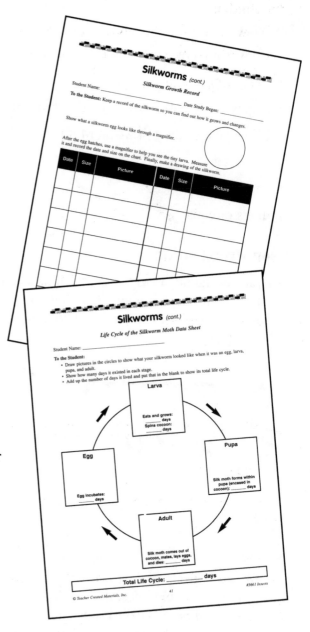

## Closure

- Have the students add the drawing of the pupa to their Life Cycle charts and Silkworm Growth Records.

- After one cocoon is completely unwound, help the students measure its length. Rewind it on another spool or as it is measured.

## *Life Cycle of the Silkworm Moth Data Sheet*

Student Name: _____

**To the Student:**
- Draw pictures in the circles to show what your silkworm looked like when it was an egg, larva, pupa, and adult.
- Show how many days it existed in each stage.
- Add up the number of days it lived and put that in the blank to show its total life cycle.

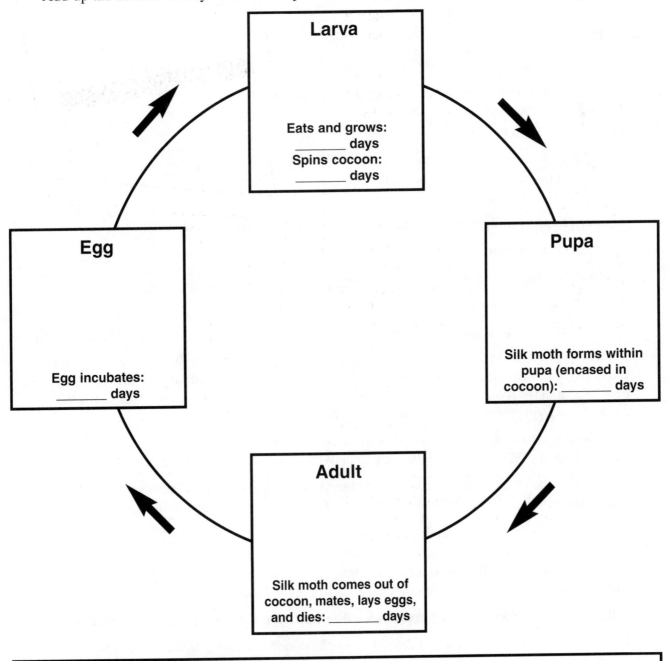

**Larva**

Eats and grows:
_____ days
Spins cocoon:
_____ days

**Egg**

Egg incubates:
_____ days

**Pupa**

Silk moth forms within pupa (encased in cocoon): _____ days

**Adult**

Silk moth comes out of cocoon, mates, lays eggs, and dies: _____ days

**Total Life Cycle: _____ days**

# Silkworms (cont.)

## *Pupa to Adult*

**Overview:** *Students will observe the silkworm become an adult moth.*

## Materials

- silkworm cocoons
- recording charts
- magnifiers

## Lesson Preparation

- Begin this lesson when the adult silkworm moths begin to emerge from the cocoons.
- Continue to add to the videotape, if one is being made of the life cycle of the silkworm.

## Activity

1. Have the students gather around to observe as one or more moths begin to emerge. Help students look for details as they observe the moths emerge, as well as over the next few days. Examples of what to look for are given below.

   - moths exuding a liquid which dissolves a hole in the cocoon through which they emerge
   - fluid being pumped into the wings (This may take about 15 minutes.)
   - physical features such as legs, antennae, eyes, and body
   - movement of the moths
   - moths mating and laying eggs

2. Discuss the differences between the adult moth and the larva. Explain that the silkworm moth cannot fly since its wings are too small. Tell them that long ago it had larger wings but they have been bred to have smaller wings by those who raised them over many years. This keeps the moths from flying away and makes it easier to collect their eggs.

3. Have students make detailed drawings of the adults on the Life Cycle charts and Silkworm Growth Record. Measure the adults so they may add this information to their charts.

4. Explain that the moths will not eat—in fact, they have no teeth or biting parts in their mouths. They will only live long enough to mate and for the female to lay eggs; then they die.

## Closure

- Have the students complete their Silkworm Journals by placing their drawings and charts inside a construction paper cover on which they make drawings of what they observed.
- Tell the students to write a summary of what they learned about these remarkable insects.
- Provide each student with some of the silk from the cocoon to tape into their journals.

# Going on a Bee Hunt

## *Studying Bees*

**Overview:** *Students will study bees in the wild.*

## Materials
- area of flowers
- transparency of *Anatomy of a Worker Honey Bee* (page 44)
- notepaper
- flowers with pollen on their stamens
- magnifiers
- optional: camcorder to videotape the observations to show later in class

## Activity
1. Find an area of flowers near the school where you see active bees.  Practice observing them by standing at a safe distance but close enough to see the pollen which they collected on their hind legs and, how they move into the flower for nectar.

2. Some students may be afraid of bees, especially if they have been stung.  Check to see if any of the students are allergic to bee stings.  Tell the students well before the excursion what they will do on this field trip.  Ask for volunteer adults to escort small groups of the students.

3. Show the students a video or film that has close-up pictures of bees collecting nectar. Read books about bees and use the transparency of *Anatomy of a Worker Honeybee* to familiarize students with their body parts.

4. The best time to observe bees is when it is warm and sunny.  Explain to the students that the bees will ignore them if they don't make any sudden moves. The vision of a bee is blurred and they only notice motion rather than individual images as we do.

5. Tell the students to watch how the bee moves its wings as they approach a flower.  Remind them to look for pollen sticking to their hind legs.  Tell them to listen for the buzzing sound made by the bee's wings.  Have them notice which flowers the bees enjoy most.

6. Pick some of the flowers that the bees are visiting and pass them to the students.  Have them  use magnifiers to see the stamens in the flowers. Tell them to rub their fingers over the stamens to see the pollen (often yellow) will rub off.

## Closure
- After returning to the classroom, divide the students into different groups and have them share what they saw during the trip.
- List the observations on the board for all the students to see and compare what they each saw.
- If a video was made, show it as a review of what they saw and discuss what they learned.

## Extender
- Invite a beekeeper to school to explain how he or she collects the honey and tends the hives.
- Read *The Magic School Bus Inside a Beehive* by Joanna Cole aloud and share the illustrations. It provides an excellent description of the life of bees.

# Going on a Bee Hunt *(cont.)*

## *Anatomy of a Worker Honeybee*

**These detailed pictures show the body parts of a honeybee and explain their functions.**

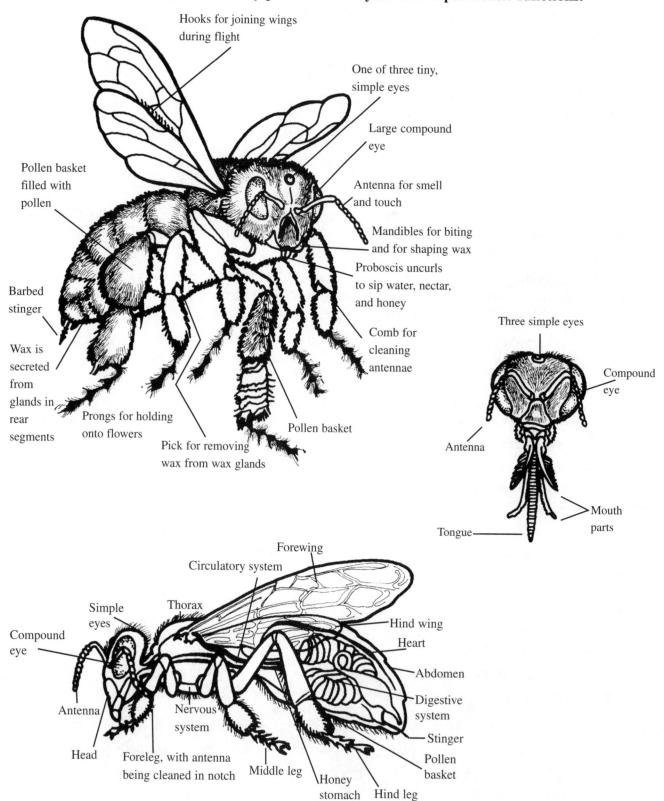

Hooks for joining wings during flight

One of three tiny, simple eyes

Large compound eye

Antenna for smell and touch

Mandibles for biting and for shaping wax

Proboscis uncurls to sip water, nectar, and honey

Comb for cleaning antennae

Pollen basket filled with pollen

Barbed stinger

Wax is secreted from glands in rear segments

Prongs for holding onto flowers

Pick for removing wax from wax glands

Pollen basket

Three simple eyes

Compound eye

Antenna

Mouth parts

Tongue

Forewing

Circulatory system

Thorax

Simple eyes

Compound eye

Antenna

Head

Nervous system

Foreleg, with antenna being cleaned in notch

Middle leg

Honey stomach

Hind leg

Hind wing

Heart

Abdomen

Digestive system

Stinger

Pollen basket

# Imaginary Insect Zoo

**Overview:** *Students will make imaginary insects which have the essential characteristics of an insect, such as six legs and three body parts.*

## Materials

- variety of items for construction of insects (e.g., pipe cleaners, egg cartons, cellophane)
- scissors
- glue gun
- white glue
- pictures of a variety of colorful and unusual insects
- copies of parent letter (page 46)
- copies of data sheet This Is My Insect (page 47)

## Lesson Preparation

- Send letters to the parents requesting their assistance in gathering materials to use in creating fanciful insects.
- Assemble a variety of materials students can use in their construction, such as cardboard, crepe paper, paint, paper clips, and other school supplies.
- Set up a hot-glue area (operated by an adult) if students need creations glued this way.
- Place colorful and unusual insect pictures on a bulletin board. Put books of insects nearby.

## Activity

1. As a post test, give the pretest Is This an Insect? that was used at the beginning of the study of insects. Have students discuss the results of the test and encourage them to tell how they can distinguish an insect from a noninsect.
2. Explain that students are going to make an insect zoo from imaginary insects that they create. Distribute the parent letter to each student and read and discuss it so they know what to collect for their insect constructions.
3. Show students the pictures of insects on the bulletin board and in books you have provided. Let them examine these to get some ideas about the materials they might need to make an insect.
4. After collecting materials, place them in a central area, permitting students to share the materials if they wish to do so. Review what makes an insect different from a noninsect.
5. Let students work on their imaginary insects. Allow sufficient time, perhaps several days.

## Closure

- Distribute copies of the data sheet This Is My Insect to students and let them complete it to tell about their creation.
- Set aside an area for the insect zoo and arrange the students' insect models in it. Put each child's description with his or her model. Have students make invitations for other classes and parents, inviting them to visit the zoo.

*Parent Letter for Insect Materials*

Date_____

### Dear Parents,

Your child has learned much about insects as our class looked at a wide variety of insects brought from areas around our houses and school grounds. We have also raised mealworms, ants, butterflies, and silkworms. Now, we are ready to create our own unique zoo of imaginary insects. We need your help in gathering the materials students can use to create their imaginary insects. Some of these are listed below:

- aluminum foil
- pipe cleaners
- thin wire
- feathers
- colored cellophane
- small buttons
- toilet tissue rolls
- egg cartons

We have looked at pictures of many different types of insects to give the students ideas. Talk with your child, asking what may be needed to make his or her insect. If you can spare extra items beyond those your child will use, they will be gratefully accepted for other students to use.

The class will begin to create the insects on_____. Please send the materials to school with your child before this date. Our Imaginary Insect Zoo should be ready for you to visit within a week after we begin construction. You will receive a notice announcing its grand opening and inviting you to visit.

Thank you for your help in enriching our study of insects.

Cordially,

_____

# Imaginary Insect Zoo *(cont.)*

## *This is My Insect*

Name: _____ Date: _____

Insect's Name: _____ .

It eats _____ .

Tell how your insect can . . .

• **smell:** _____

• **hear:** _____

• **see:** _____

• **taste:** _____

• **eat:** _____

• **move around:** _____

• **protect itself:** _____

Make a drawing to show your insect's life cycle.

# Teacher and Student Resources

## Related Books

Dorling Kindersley Publishing Company. *Big Book of Bugs.* 2001  Order online from DK. (See below.)

This is an up-close and personal book for young entomologists and all curious kids who are fascinated with bugs. Look right into a spider's eye and get tangled in its web! Marvel at the stunning pictures of teeny tiny creepy crawlies blown up to extraordinary sizes. Engaging annotations provide buggy facts and figures. Larger than life photographs of creepy crawlies include locusts, caterpillars, beetles, flies, grasshoppers, ants, praying mantis, and more!

Cole, Joanna. *The Magic School Bus Inside a Beehive.*  Scholastic, Inc. 1996.  Ms. Frizzle takes her students on another field trip adventure; this time they become bees and investigate a beehive.  They learn all about the roles of bees in the hive and how they find their food and tend the larvae.

Woelflein, L. *The Ultimate Pop Up Bug Book.* 1993  **http://popupbooks.net/BookU/U2.html**

This book depicts and describes various interesting insects— their growth, societies, eating habits, and survival mechanisms.  Included are five intricate double-page pop-ups, with tab-mechanicals, lift-flaps, a turn-wheel, a slat-picture, a cricket sound-chip, and a scratch-and-sniff.

Young, Ruth M. *Science/Literature Unit: Magic School Bus® Inside a Beehive.* Teacher Created Resources, Inc., 1997.  The activity-oriented lessons in this unit bring to life the field trip taken by Ms. Frizzle and her students as they visit a beehive, by becoming bees.  Other lessons in the unit help students learn about other insects including, ants, silkworms, and butterflies.

## Suppliers of Science Materials

**Carolina Biological**  (800) 334-5551  **http://www.carolina.com/**

**Delta Education**   (800) 282-9560.  Request a catalog of materials or order online at their Website.
**http://www.delta-education.com/corp/info/ordernow.html**

Supplies books, videos, magnifying "bug boxes", ant farms, and other insect materials.

**Dorling Kindersley (DK)**  **http://usstore.dk.com/shop/**

Offers materials about insects online including *3–D Insect,* a book for ages 8 - 14, and an insect video. Also featured are books from the DK Explorer series such as *Insects and Butterflies and Moths.*

**Insect Lore**  (800) LIVE BUG  or **www.insectlore.com.**  Request a free catalog.

Supplies painted lady butterfly larvae, ant farms, silkworm eggs, live ladybird beetles, and videos.

**National Science Teachers Association (NSTA)**

**http://www.nsta.org/**  or the online catalog of materials at **http://store.nsta.org/**

This outstanding organization, founded in 1944, has a membership 53,000, which includes science teachers, science supervisors, administrators, scientists, and business and industry. Members receive  a monthly professional journal, the bimonthly NSTA Reports, discounts at the regional and national conventions and annual catalog of materials.